BENEATH THE SURFACE

Beneath The Surface

K.N. S.J.P.

Epic Fiction

CONTENTS

~ 8 ~

Finding Jeanine

~ 9 ~

Reunited

$$\sim 1 \sim$$

A FAMILIAR FACE

The sun shined brightly, casting a warm glow on Jeanine as she walked up the walkway to Dreams Studios. An old storage unit company turned into apartments to help house low-income families. As she approached the entrance, she noticed a familiar face. She squinted, trying to get a better look. Her heart began to race and excitement filled her veins as she got closer to the lady.

"Rachel???"

Jeanine called out. The lady seemed to hear her but she quickly turned and scurried off around the corner. Jeanine frowned, puzzled by the woman's behavior.

Hmmm, maybe that wasn't her. I hope I didn't scare that lady. If I see her again, I will apologize.
She thought, but she was certain that it was an old friend of hers.

It was an uneventful evening at work with the gentle ebb and flow of routine tasks and familiar faces. The atmosphere within the converted storage units was filled with subdued energy as residents went about their daily lives, each encapsulated within their private spaces. As Jeanine walked through the well-lit hallways adorned with faded artwork and the occasional flickering fluorescent light, she couldn't shake the thought of seeing the mysterious lady who resembled her friend. She wondered why Rachel would avoid her, they were such good friends at one point in their lives. After finishing her shift, she hurried home, looking forward to some much-needed rest and relaxation.

Jeanine sighed with relief as she unlocked the door to her cozy apartment. The welcoming familiar scent of home enveloped the space, inviting her to unwind. She eagerly shed her work clothes, slipped into the comfort of her favorite loungewear, and made her way to the living room. Jeanine sank into the plush cushions of her thrifted, well-worn armchair. Taking a few deep breaths, she allowed herself a moment to close her eyes, hoping to quiet the whirlwind of thoughts that haunted her throughout the evening. The rhythmic ticking of the clock on the wall served as a gentle backdrop to her contemplation, enticing her to sleep.

The next day came as fast as it went. Jeanine stretched her limbs as the soft glow of morning light gently filtered through her bedroom window. She felt refreshed and determined to have a great day. Optimism danced in her mind as the warm shower water cascaded over her, washing away the remnants of yesterday, and embracing her with revitalization.

Dressed in her favorite outfit, Jeanine adorned herself with a silver pendant, a cherished keepsake from her childhood. She quietly squealed with delight when her coffee pot timer beeped. A steaming fresh cup of coffee was just what she needed to complete her morning ritual. With a spring in her step, she quickly made her way to the kitchen where the aroma of freshly brewed coffee filled the air.

Pouring the hot liquid into her favorite travel mug, Jeanine inhaled deeply, savoring the rich, earthy notes that mingled with hints of nuttiness and subtle undertones of dark chocolate. The scent whispered of distant, sacred lands and the painstaking labor that went into each roasted bean as their natural oils released their full-bodied aroma. As she took a cautious first sip, the taste spoke of possibilities of the new energy and inspiration that awaited her as the caffeine coursed through her veins, awakening her mind and sharpening her thoughts. With her coffee and books in hand, Jeanine embraced the day, ready to seize every opportunity that lay before her.

A symphony of voices filled the air as Jeanine entered the bustling lecture hall. Each conversation was an instrument in the grand orchestra of learning. Her fellow classmates' faces were alive with a mix of enthusiasm and curiosity as they clustered together in small groups, exchanging ideas and preparing for the day's lesson. It was a vibrant atmosphere as she navigated her way through the sea of animated discussions, catching snippets of intriguing conversations and shared laughter. Taking her seat, Jeanine felt a sense of belonging wash over her. The familiar surroundings wrapped her in a comforting cocoon of academia.

"Hey, Jeanine! Ready for another day of learning?" Evelyn greeted her with a warm smile.

"Absolutely! How are you doing today?"

"Chile, you won't believe what happened to me last night!"

She plopped down in the seat next to Jeanine with a playful twinkle in her eyes.

"What happened?" Jeanine chuckled.

She loved talking to Evelyn, there was never a dull moment when she came to class. Evelyn Bennett was a vivacious woman in her mid-fifties with a zest for life that was contagious. Her radiant smile and infectious laughter could light up the entire lecture hall, effortlessly melting away any nearby tension. Jeanine admired Evelyn's youthful spirit and her ability to embrace her age with grace and confidence. She reminded Jeanine of her favorite aunt who had passed away when Jeanine was younger. Despite the age gap, their conversations always flowed seamlessly.

"Well," Evelyn took a deep breath.

"I was peacefully enjoying my evening stories, sipping on a cup of herbal tea when suddenly, Biscuits and Gravy, went on a wild rampage!" Her hands flailed and her eyes widened as she told the story.

Jeanine stifled a laugh, picturing the scene. Evelyn always shared her crazy experiences with her cats, Biscuits, and Gravy.

"They decided that my herb garden was their personal playground! I said, "The devil is a lie!" and got my shoe and chase their butts right on up out of my chamomile and lavender!"

Jeanine couldn't help but burst into laughter, imagining Evelyn running through her house with a shoe, chasing cats.

"I would have spanked their butts too if I could catch 'em!"

"I bet! I can picture you chasing after them! Herbs just flying everywhere!"

Evelyn joined Jeanine and nearby eavesdroppers in laughter.

"They keep me young. I always have to expect the unexpected with them, even if it means a few crushed herbs along the way!"

"I'm glad you found humor in all that chaos! I would have put them out!" Jeanine laughter subsided to a smile.

"Good morning class!"

The room abruptly hushed as the professor made her way into the room.

"Today we will be discussing the history of herbalism and how it has evolved over the centuries."

Jeanine settled into her seat, her mind filled with anticipation for the lesson. She scribbled notes, capturing every detail and insight shared by the professor. Her words painted vivid pictures of ancient civilizations, traditional healing practices, and the transformative power of plants. But amidst the engaging lecture, Jeanine's thoughts kept drifting back to the mysterious lady she had seen the day before. She couldn't shake the feeling that it was her old friend. Her mind wandered back to the days of their carefree youth when she and Rachel dreamed of conquering the world together. But somewhere along the way, their paths diverged, leading to an unexpected separation that neither of them had expected.

Lost in her thoughts, Jeanine was jolted back to reality by the buzz of her watch alarm, signaling the end of class. She packed her belongings slowly, her mind still grappling with unanswered questions.

"See you tomorrow, Evelyn."

Jeanine waved before walking off. Stepping outside, the sunlight gently kissed her cheeks and wrapped its rays around her reminding her of her grandmother's loving arms. Memories of lazy afternoons spent nestled in her grandmother's lap, listening to old stories, and the steady beat of her noni's heart came flooding back to her. Tears filled her eyes as she remembered her grandparents' unwavering support and guidance throughout her life. She sighed as she took a deep breath and proceeded to her car.

Looking to her left, much to her surprise, was the lady from the night before. She was standing under a tree in the distance, just at the edge of Jeanine's vision. Her breath caught in her throat as she blinked her eyes repeatedly straining to get a clearer view. The mysterious lady seemed to sense Jeanine's gaze, slowly turning toward her, their eyes meeting for a fleeting moment.

"Jeanine! Jeanine!"

Jeanine spun around quickly seeing Evelyn waving papers in the air, briskly shuffling across the parking lot.

"You forgot your handouts!"

She frantically looked back to the woman but she was gone. Jeanine's heart raced as she tried to visually locate the woman, but she was nowhere in sight. Frustrated, she turned back to Evelyn, thanking her for the handouts.

Driving to work, Jeanine shook her head, trying to rid herself of the paranoid thoughts. Who was this woman? Was it really Rachel? Was she following her or was it a coincidence?

~ 2 ~

HOT COFFEE

The questions swirled in Jeanine's mind as she waited in the drive-through line at her favorite coffee shop, Ky's Kafe. Doubts and insecurities flooded her thoughts. What if she was wrong? What if she was right, but Rachel didn't want to reconnect?

"Ugh!" she grunted as she looked over the menu.

"Heeeey! What are you having today?"

Ky, her favorite barista, excitedly greeted her at the window.

"Hey, girl... I guess just the regular..."

"You're so boring! One black coffee with a double shot of espresso coming up!" Ky playfully rolled her eyes.

She chuckled at her coffee shop friend, wondering why they never hung out. Their interactions had always been confined to exchanging pleasantries over coffee orders. Throughout the years, Jeanine developed a tendency to keep to herself, finding solace in her own company rather than navigating the complexities of form-ing deep, meaningful connections. Whenever she thought about expanding her social circle, she quickly talked herself out of it. The allure of meeting new people was overshadowed by her past experiences with difficult people. It just wasn't worth the trouble. Jeanine was relieved Ky never invited her to go out.

"Hey, here you go, hun! Now, you know I would normally hold up this line to chat with you but we are swamped! Hugo called out again! I am about to fire his ass!" She laughed, wiping sweat from her head.

"No worries! We will catch up next time! Muah!"

Jeanine blew her a kiss as she pulled away, her mind teetering between hope and uncertainty. The sightings of the familiar face lingered in her thoughts as she parked her car at work, she took a moment to collect herself before stepping out. She couldn't let the mysterious woman distract her from her duties.

As she made her way to the storage unit entrance, Jeanine's thoughts consumed her so completely, she failed to notice the commotion ahead. Suddenly, someone burst through the double doors and right into her, knocking her books and coffee out of her hands.

"Ahhhh! Sssss! Ahhhh!"

Jeanine fell to her knees cradling her hands and the stinging spot on her leg where the hot coffee spilled, searing her skin.

"I'm sorry! I'm sorry! I'm so sorry!"

The lady said repeatedly, her voice filled with genuine remorse. She scrambled to gather the scattered papers and books and attempted to salvage what remained of the spilled coffee.

"It's okay, It's okay, really, I'm okay..."

Jeanine winced, taking a deep breath, trying to steady herself as the pain gradually subsided.

"Oh my gosh! Oh my gosh! Please don't sue me! My mother is going to kill me! I am sooo sorry!"

"Heeey, calm down, it's really okay, I will be okay!"

Jeanine looked up at the lady, her eyes filled with a mix of discomfort and understanding. She rubbed the lady's shoulders, she was shaking profusely.

"Calm down, okay? Accidents happen."

The lady let out a shaky sigh of relief, wiping tears from her face as her frantic movements slowed. She slowly looked up, handing Jeanine her books, careful not to touch her burned hands. Jeanine fell back in shock as she locked eyes with the woman.

"Rachel??? IT IS YOU! Oh my gosh!" Her eyes widened in disbelief.

"Uh, I... uh, you must have me confused with someone else! I uh, I umm, I am running late! So sorry!"

Rachel stammered, her gaze darted nervously, avoiding direct eye contact. She quickly covered her face with a scarf and ran off, tripping over the sidewalk as she desperately tried to escape the conversation.

"RACHEL!!!"

Jeanine's heart sank as she yelled after, she was in total disbelief as she watched Rachel make record time down the block and around the corner.

Did she think I was going to chase her? Should I chase her?

"Damn, that girl is fast! What the hell was that about???" Jeanine was more confused than ever.

That night, she tossed and turned in her bed thinking about Rachel. She searched her mind for more memories of their time together but couldn't remember much. She remembered eating lunch with Rachel at school every day but everything else was a blur. It had been like 15 years since she last saw her, so much had happened since then. Feeling restless, Jeanine dug out the dusty memorabilia box she kept at the top of her closet. It was filled with old pictures and keepsakes from her childhood.

"We looked happy…"

She sorted through the photos, smiling at a few familiar faces, wondering where everyone was now. Unfortunately, seeing the pictures didn't help more memories resurface. After a few hours of trying to piece together the past, she blew out her lavender, jade, palo santo candle, snuggled up next to Bruce, her oversized teddy bear, and went to bed.

~ 3 ~

THE SEARCH

Jeanine didn't see Rachel over the next week. She wondered what and why Rachel was hiding, she hoped she was okay. Jeanine found herself constantly thinking about her lost friend. Unable to bear the uncertainty any longer, she decided to take matters into her own hands and do some investigating.

"Hey, have you seen this lady?"

She held up a picture of her long-lost friend to the front desk clerk. He gave her a funny look as he shuffled through some mail.

"Well, hi to you too!!! And uh, no... Not many little girls live here."

"Sorry, hi... I don't mean to be rude, I'm just on a mission to find someone. She's not a little girl anymore" Jeanine took a deep breath.

"Just look at the face and picture the adult version..."

"I'm not that good with faces. I see so many, they all seem to blur after a while. Sorry, kiddo."

"Okay, Thanks anyway..."

"Thanks for nothing." She mumbled under her breath as she walked away.

Over the next few weeks, during her breaks and after work, Jeanine approached her coworkers, neighbors, and residents of the building, striking up conversations about Rachel. One afternoon, she ran into a longtime resident of Dream Studio.

"Hey, Bree!"

"Hey, girl, I haven't seen you in a while. You alright?"

"Yeah, I am good. You know how life can get..."

"Totally. What are you up to?"

"Well, I have been looking for an old friend of mine. She used to live here, her name is Rachel."

"Hmm, Rachel? Girl, there are so many people that come through here, it's hard to keep up with everyone. I think I remember someone by that name who moved out a few months ago. She was tall, blonde, and always wore some funky-looking glasses, right?"

"Uh, no. Rachel is a redhead..." Jeanine heart dropped.

"Oh, sorry... Well, if I hear anything I will definitely let you know!" Bree gave Jeanine a hug.
"Good luck finding your friend."

"Thanks, take care."

Jeanine leaned up against the wall and took a deep breath. She was so tired of hitting dead ends.

"Hey, love! Sorry to eavesdrop, but did I hear you say you are looking for Rachel?"

"Uh, YES!" Jeanine stood straight up with hopeful eyes.

"Do you know her?"

"Yeah, Rachel is great! We used to hang out a lot but a few weeks ago she just vanished and I haven't been able to find her. Last I heard, she got a job at a bookstore downtown. She loves books. I went down there a few times but always seemed to miss her. I am starting to think she's avoiding me" The lady shrugged.

"Oh, wow! Thank you so much! What bookstore?" Jeanine felt optimistic.

"It's called Pages over on Elm Street."

With a renewed sense of purpose, Jeanine thanked the lady and left the building in a hurry. She briskly walked toward Elm Street, excitement in her footsteps. Reaching Pages Bookstore, Jeanine pushed the door open and scanned the bustling bookshop, hoping to get a glimpse of Rachel. Searching the aisles, side rooms, and restrooms, there was no sign of her friend. Uncertainty crept back into her thoughts. She approached the counter, where a friendly bookseller stood, arranging a stack of novels.

"Excuse me, is there anyone who works here by the name Rachel?" Jeanine flashed a reluctant smile.

"Rachel? Hmm, we don't have anyone by that name on our staff. Are you sure you have the right place?"

"Yes, I was told she works here or worked here. Are you sure, can you double check please?"

"I'm sorry Miss, but I have been working here for years and our staff isn't that big. If we had a Rachel, I would know."

"Oh, ok. Well, sorry to bother you."

"I'm sorry I couldn't be more help. If you need any book recommendations or assistance with anything else, please don't hesitate to ask."
"Thanks."

Leaving the bookstore, Jeanine felt disappointed and confused, her spirits sank as her search for Rachel turned up empty once again. Despite her best efforts, the trail had grown cold. It had been almost a month and she hadn't found any valid information about Rachel. Feeling frustrated and hopeless, she decided it was time to let go and shift her focus back to her own life. As she placed the photographs back in the box, she couldn't help but feel a tinge of sadness. Jeanine closed the box and placed it back in the closet.

Well, I tried... I wonder what she's up to? Why is she hiding and acting so strangely? Welp, not my business! Let me get my work done.

She thought while pouring a cup of peppermint tea. Winding down for the evening, she read over notes for tomorrow's test until she fell asleep.

Months passed and life resumed its familiar rhythm. Jeanine threw herself into her studies, work, and her hobbies. She did her best to keep thoughts of Rachel at bay, convincing herself that it was time to move on. But deep down, a small part of her still longed for closure.

~ 4 ~

DEAR JEANINE

"Ugh, Monday already?"

Jeanine groaned, rolling over and placing her pillow over her head. It felt like she had just fallen asleep. She typically didn't wake up this early but she left her charger at work and had to make a quick stop there before class.

As Jeanine arrived at Dream Studios, she was taken aback to see Rachel standing out front, smoking a cigarette. She hesitated as she cautiously approached her friend.

"Rach?"

Jeanine spoke softly. Rachel jumped at the sound of her name, quickly pulling her hoodie over her face and turning her back.

"You got the wrong person."

"Come on, Rach, I know it's you. I have been looking for you. I, I uh, I was just hoping to catch up with you sometime. If that's okay?"

"I... I... I don't think that's a good idea...?"

Rachel turned and looked Jeanine up and down, shivering as she took another drag of her cigarette. It was clear she was grappling with her own internal struggles.

"Have I done something to offend you? We used to be such good friends..." Jeanine's voice quivered looking into Rachel's tired eyes.

"You really wouldn't understand."

"Wouldn't understand what?"

"I..." Rachel paused, her eyes darting around as she noticed some men approaching in the distance.

"I'm sorry, I gotta go."

Jeanine's heart dropped as she watched Rachel hastily wrap her oversized sweater jacket around herself tightly and hurriedly walked away.

"Well... ok... Take care!"

Jeanine waved at her but she never turned around.

"Maybe it's drugs..."
She murmured to herself, shrugging her shoulders as she entered the building.

Three weeks later, Jeanine received a text from her mother letting her know she had received a package but it didn't say who it was from. She decided to pick it up after class that day. Sitting in her car, she stared at the unassuming package, her mind swirling with questions.

"This is weird... What if it's a bomb? Why would someone try to blow me up though?"

She laughed nervously, took a deep breath, and pried the corners of the box back. To her surprise, she found a collection of items inside - a letter, pictures, and drawings from a young Rachel.

"Wow, I can't believe she kept all this!"

As she shuffled through the nostalgic contents, she felt a rush of emotions, her eyes filled with tears. She took a moment to compose herself before reaching for the letter. With trembling hands, Jeanine unfolded the letter.

Dear Jeanine,

I hope this letter finds you well. Let me start off by saying, I'm so sorry. How I treated you has been weighing heavily on me lately. I have been cold and rude. I just see you with your beautiful skin, well-done hair, and toned body and I get jealous and envious. You always look so well put together, life turned out really great for you, huh? I wish my life turned out differently. We were such good friends as kids, best friends! So... I feel that it's only fair for me to share with you what happened and why I moved away.

Sigh

I guess things took a turn for the worse about 12 years ago. My family was living a decent life until my dad lost his job due to company layoffs. Even though my mother made good money as a nurse, they were still unable to make ends meet and eventually fell behind in rent. We tried to find a new place to live but the cost of living was too high, and we couldn't afford it. We stayed in our home as long as possible until we were eventually evicted. Losing the house caused a lot of problems between my parents. They started fighting all the time. My father ended up leaving my mother for another woman months later and we were left to fend for ourselves. He has since remarried and is living upstate somewhere. We haven't heard from him in like 5 years. We have been struggling to find a way out of here but I can barely make enough money to keep me, my sister and my mom fed most days. But I am doing my best to stay hopeful.

Well... That's how we came to live at Dream Studios Storage. I have been so ashamed and embarrassed to be seen here, I hide my face as much as possible! I was so shocked and embarrassed the first time you noticed me. That is why I took off running when you called my name. Maybe one day we can reconnect when things are better for me. But for now, I think it's best that you not be seen with the likes of me! I hope your hand and leg are okay from the coffee burn! Thanks for not suing me!!! Everyone is suing everybody nowadays over the smallest things in the hopes of a come-up ya know... It's really sad. Just last week a guy had a nosebleed and accidentally got blood on a lady's shoes. The lady sued him for a new pair of shoes and WON! The world is crazy man! So, I just do my best to keep my head down and stay out of the way ya know.

I'm glad your life worked out so well! I always wondered what happened to you. I looked you up on Facebook once but couldn't find you. I don't have one of those fancy phones that allows you to download apps so I am pretty disconnected from social media. Sometimes I go to the library and get on the computers but seeing everyone from high school doing so well just makes me depressed so I decided to stop looking.

Please don't come looking for me and I hope this doesn't come off as harsh but if you see me, can you just pretend like you don't know me... It's too much for me to bear right now. I'm so, so, so, sorry Jeanie... I wish you all the best! If I don't see you again in this lifetime, maybe our paths will cross in the next!

~Love Rach

~ 5 ~

REGRET

Jeanine was in tears reading about what happened to Rachel over the years and a little hurt too that she wanted nothing to do with her. And if she was being honest, she was upset. Rachel judged her without even knowing her story. Jeanine's life hadn't been perfect either but she did her best to understand Rachel's perspective.

"I guess..." Jeanine murmured.

She sighed, wiped her tears, tossed the box in the backseat, and drove off. Jeanine's heart was heavy as she drove to work. It was a beautiful sunny day outside, the sky was clear and a warm breeze blew through the car window. The roads blurred as she navigated her way to work, her mind consumed by thoughts of Rachel's letter. Jeanine was too lost in her emotions to appreciate the splendid weather. Her sadness cast a shadow over the sunshine, clouding her perception of the world around her. As she parked her car at work, she rested her head on the steering wheel and took several deep breaths, attempting to calm herself. As she reached to open her car door, Jeanine looked over and saw a familiar face standing outside the front entrance.

"Ugh! Of course!" She muttered.

"Of all the days for Rachel to be outside!!! I haven't seen her in weeks! Why now?!? Ugh!"

She hit her steering wheel in frustration and reclined her seat back. Jeanine sat in her car and waited for Rachel to disappear around the corner, then she quickly hurried inside.

Days later, Rachel sat alone lost in deep thought. Her letter to Jeanine replayed relentlessly in her mind. The weight of her worlds sunk deeper and deeper with each passing minute. She couldn't help but wonder if she made a mistake. Did she push away the one person from her past who genuinely cared about her?

"I hope I didn't hurt her feelings..."

"What's that hun?" Her mom questioned from across the room.

"Oh, nothing, just thinking about the letter I wrote to Jeanine."

"You wrote her a letter??? I have been meaning to ask you if you saw her. I thought she looked familiar, so I went up and spoke to her a few weeks ago. She is such a sweet young lady."

"Yeah..."

"What did you write? Why do you think you hurt her feelings?" Christine sat next to her daughter on the bed, her voice filled with concern..

"Well, I pretty much told her to not speak to me again and to pretend like she didn't know me if she saw me..." Rachel sighed and fidgeted with her hands.

"Why in the world would you tell her something like that??? Did she do something to you?" Her mother was shocked, she didn't know her daughter to be so mean-spirited.

"I'm just embarrassed to be seen here! I am sick of this place and the looks I get from people when I walk outside! Everyone judges me before they even get to know me! I am sick of it!" Rachel threw her head back on the couch.

"You're the one being judgemental... The world doesn't revolve around you sweetheart. You should do a little research while you are walking around here feeling bad for yourself."

Christine patted her daughter's leg, got up, and walked across the room to the kitchenette.

"What does that mean?" Rachel looked at her mother puzzled, she wasn't expecting that response.

"Oh, nothing... You got it all figured out..."

"MOOOOM! Tell me! What are you talking about!"

Christine poured herself a glass of water and smiled at Rachel. She lived for teachable moments with her children. She grabbed a snack bag of pretzels as she watched her daughter squirm, begging her to tell her what she knew. Halfway through the bag, she had enough.

"Okay, okay! Simmer down." Christine pointed to the loveseat. Rachel went and flopped down in frustration.

"Have you ever noticed Jeanine's clothes?"

"Her clothes? No, not really... She always wears this really cute peacoat. Why???"

"Well, when I first saw Jeanine about a month ago, I was on my way to speak to her when I was stopped by Kathy, telling me some crazy story about Doug again. I noticed Jeanine was wearing the uniform of the employees here. So, after I was done talking to Kathy, I went to the front desk and asked for her. They said no one worked there by that name. This puzzled me so I thought maybe they were mistaken and I went back the next day and asked for the manager."

"Uh-huh, and then what happened???" Rachel was up on her knees in anticipation.

~ 6 ~

WELL, THIS IS MY STOP

"Well, he wasn't there, so I left my name and number for him to give me a call. I also began to think maybe it wasn't her, maybe it was just someone who just looked like her, right? Days passed and still no call from the manager so I just forgot about it, ya know. Then BOOM! There she was! Driving up to the building one day. I waited at the front door to speak to her. She was so shocked and surprised to see me as I was her! I asked her how long she had been working here, she said almost three years now! I was surprised we had never run into her in all this time. She said she usually the back door. We talked for a few minutes, I gave her a hug and I haven't seen her since but I really don't get out much, ya know..."

"Why do I feel like there is more to this story? What are you not telling me?" Rachel could tell by her mother's face that she was holding back. Christine took a sip of her water and ate a few more pretzels.

"MOM!!"

"Okay! So, the next day, guess who calls me?"

"Whoooo???" Rachel was starting to get annoyed. She hates it when her mom has a juicy story and drags out the details. Christine laughed. She was truly getting a kick out of her daughter's frustration.

"The MANAGER! I asked him about Jeanine and he said he didn't have anyone who worked here by that name either! I described her to him and he was like "Ooooh! JJ? I always forget her full name is Jeanine!" He went on to tell me that she in fact did not work there but she lived in the back of the building. She tragically lost her husband and children a few years ago in a car accident and has been trying to rebuild a life for herself ever since. She wears the uniform as a disguise so no one knows she lives here."

"What the fuck Mom!!!" Rachel jumped up, her eyes wide with disbelief.

"Watch your mouth!!!" Christine waved a finger, scolding her.

"WHY ARE YOU JUST NOW TELLING ME THIS!?!?!" She paced the floor, throwing her hands in the air.

"I'm getting old girl, I just forgot! You are always on the go and coming home so late, we barely have time to talk." Christine shrugged her shoulders and began washing dishes.

"Oh my gosh! I had no idea she was going through so tragic! I couldn't image going through that! I feel terrible! She is just as alone as I am!"

"Well, guess I'm chopped liver!" Christine crossed her arms.

"Mom! You know what I mean!" Rachel stared at her mother.

"I know, sweetheart. That's why one should never assume any-thing. Sometimes, we only see the surface of a person's life, and there is so much more beneath the surface. We shouldn't judge on appearances alone. It's a lesson we all have to learn in life."

"Do you know which apartment she lives in?"

"No, he wouldn't give me that information. He already told me too much but I told him she was a friend of the family so he gave me the icing on the cake, ya know."

Rachel bolted out the door and headed to the nearest bus stop. She anxiously caught 4 buses to Jeanine's mother's house where she had previously left the package. During the bus rides, Rachel's mind buzzed with thoughts of Jeanine. Memories from their child-hood friendship flooded back, and she couldn't help but wonder how their paths had diverged so drastically. Before her final stop, the rhythmic motion of the bus mirrored the racing beat of her heart and lulled her into a drowsy state. Her eyelids grew heavy, and before she knew it, she dozed off.

Rachel looked out the window and saw Jeanine standing on the corner. She looked around in a daze, her heart starting to panic as she realized she missed her stop. Frantically, she gathered her belongings and rushed to the front of the bus, pleading with the bus driver to let her off.

"Are you alright dear?" A little old lady nudged Rachel's arm.

Suddenly, Rachel's eyes fluttered open and she was jolted back to reality. She looked around and realized she had not missed her stop after all.

"Uh, yeah, I'm ok," Rachel assured the lady.

"You were yelling in your sleep. You might want to get that checked. You know I knew a good doctor once. His name was... hmm, was it Charles? No, no... Do you remember? Wait! It was Dr. Stevenson! Now that was a GOOD man and a GREAT doctor! You should have him check you out dear...." The little old lady ranted on and on.

Rachel's eyes widened, bewildered at the lady's unexpected trip down memory lane. She nodded politely, unsure of how to respond, as she mentally shook off remnants of her dream. The bus continued to rumble along its route, the familiar sights and sounds reassuring her that she hadn't strayed off course. The little old lady rambled on and on, oblivious to Rachel's annoyance with her. As the bus approached her intended destination, Rachel gathered her belongings and pulled the bell.

"Well, this is my stop." Rachel stood and squeezed past the lady who had invited herself to sit next to her.

"Oh, okay, dear. Don't forget to go see Dr. Stevenson! He will fix ya right up!" The lady yelled after her.

~ 7 ~

PLEASE DON'T BE DEAD

As Rachel approached Jeanine's mother's house, she took a deep breath, preparing herself for the conversation ahead. She banged on the door profusely, her knuckles tapping harshly against the wood. She could hear muffled movement inside, and her impatience grew with each passing second. Finally, the door swung open, and Ms. Paulette, Jeanine's mother, stood there with worried eyes and a baseball bat.

"Is everything alright out there? Is there a fire?" she asked, with a death grip on the bat.

"Uh, yes. Everything is fine, Ms. Paulette! It's me, Rachel!!! I don't know if you remember me but, Jeanine and I were good friends when we were kids. I played over here all the time!"

Ms. Paulette looked Rachel up and down. She had aged significantly over the years. The once vibrant young woman was now frail and huddled over.

"R... Rachel baby? Is that really you? We always wondered what happened to you! You and that red hair just getting everywhere!" Her voice was cracked and strained.

"Yes, it's me, Ms. Paulette," Jeanine was relieved she remembered.

"Come on in baby. Can I get you something to drink? You look parched."

"No, thank you. I would really love to stay and talk but I was wondering if you knew how I could reach Jeanine?"

"Well, she so busy nowadays, it's hard to say where she is. They just turned her cellular device off the other day for non-payment so I can't call her... You know she lives over to them storage unit apartments now. I told her she could come live back home but she is determined to make it on her own... These churren so hard-headed! How's ya momma doing Rachel?"

"My mother is well. What's Jeanine's apartment number???"

She followed Ms. Paulette to the living room. Rachel was trying not to rush her but Ms. Paulette was talking so slowly and she was on a mission.

"I think I have it written down somewhere, hold on a minute..."

Rachel paced the living room as Ms. Paulette inched her way down the hall. After about 10 minutes Rachel called out.

"Ms. Paulette...?"

No one answered.

"Ms. Paulette???" She spoke a little louder.

"Ugh! I hope she's okay…"

Rachel continued pacing the floor, she wasn't sure if she should go and check on her. After about five more minutes she decided to go and check on the elderly woman.

"Well, she did invite me in, so, technically, I'm not trespassing…" She nervously conversed with herself.

As she tiptoed down the hall, her childhood memories of playing in that house came flooding back. The creaking floorboards whispered echoes of being scolded by Jeanine's mother to stop running in the house. Rachel smiled warmly looking at the family photographs that lined the walls. She remembered her first time eating homemade fried chicken, yams, and collard greens, she didn't want to ever eat her own mother's cooking again. As she reached the doorway of what used to be Ms. Paulette's room, she paused for a moment before peeking in.

"Ms. Paulette?"

Rachel slowly peeked around the corner. Inside the room was dimly lit, the curtains drawn shut, casting a soft glow over the familiar furniture. Ms. Paulette was lying motionless across the bed.

Oh my gosh! Please don't be dead, please don't be dead!

Just as Rachel started to panic, Ms. Paulette let out a loud snore.

Oh, thank god she's not dead!

Relieved, Rachel chuckled to herself, her heart pounding heavily through her chest.

"Ms. Paulette??? Ms. Paulette???" She spoke softly, nudging her arm gently, to not startle her too abruptly. Ms. Paulette slowly opened her eyes and yawned.

"Hey, baby, you hungry?" She said with her eyes barely open.

"It's me Rachel, Ms. Paulette. You were looking for Jeanine's apartment number for me..."

"Rachel, baby? Is that really you?"

"Yes, Ms. Paulette... It's me, Rachel. I am looking for Jeanine. I left that box for her a few weeks ago. Do you remember?"

"You know you got that red hair all over my house, chile!"

~ 8 ~

FINDING JEANINE

Rachel sat in quiet disbelief at Ms. Paulette's senile state. Speechless, she pursed her lips together in frustration.

"So, you the one left that box for Jenny? I don't know what you said but it sure made her cry. Ya'll is too old to be fightin' now..."

"We are not fighting Ms. Paulette... Do you know her apartment number?"

"You know she lives over to that storage place now, right"

Rachel leaned her head back and took a deep breath. It was apparent Ms. Paulette was having memory problems in her old age.

"Yes, I know Ms. Paulette. Dooo... Yooou... Remember... Jeanine's... Aaa..part..ment... Nuuum...ber...?"

"Oh, yes. Everything for Jeanine is right there."

She pointed at the door. Rachel walked over and looked behind the bedroom door. Her eyes widened as she discovered a whiteboard full of messages, upcoming appointment reminders, sticky notes, emergency numbers, and all of Jeanine's information. Rachel's heart skipped a beat with excitement. She grabbed a pen and paper from the dresser and wrote down Jeanine's details making sure not to miss any crucial details.

"Thank you, Ms. Paulette! Thank you!!!" Rachel exclaimed.

Unable to contain her excitement she leaned down and gave her a kiss on the cheek and rushed down the hall and out the door.

"They turned off her cellular device the other day, for non-payment..."

Ms. Paulette faintly called out to Rachel as she drifted back to sleep. Rachel sprinted down the street, making her way back to the bus stop. She checked the bus schedule anxiously, hoping it would arrive soon. Time seemed to stretch as she impatiently watched the minutes tick by on her watch. Finally, the bus arrived. Rachel hurried on board, finding a seat near the front. The journey back to the storage units felt like forever. She stared out the window lost in her thoughts as the bus traversed the winding street and made multiple transfers. She watched the cityscape pass by, her mind filled with thoughts of Jeanine. It took her all night to get back to Dream Studios, but she knew the trip was worth it. Jumping off the bus, she was exhausted, but the adrenaline coursing through her veins kept her moving. She flew up three flights of stairs and down the hall, her footsteps echoing loudly. With each step, Rachel's excitement grew. Finally arriving at Jeanine's front door, she banged on the door enthusiastically.

Rachel apprehensively waited for a response. She listened intently for any sign of movement from inside the unit. Finally, she heard the sound of footsteps approaching.

"WHAT THE HELL IS GOING ON??? DO YOU KNOW WHAT TIME IT IS???" A man's voice yelled angrily from the other side.

"Sorry... Uh, sorry to bother you! I am looking for Jeanine!" Rachel paused, startled by the man's angry outburst.

"AIN'T NO JEANINE HERE!!!" the man retorted, his tone sharp and unwavering.

"Umm, I hear she goes by JJ now, is there someone named JJ here???"

"AIN'T NO JJ, NO JENNY, NO JESSICA!!! NOW GET THE HELL AWAY FROM MY DOOR!!!" he bellowed, his anger growing.

Rachel winced at the man's irate response. She took a step back from the door, looking at the paper confused, unsure of what to do next. Had she made a mistake? She is sure she wrote everything down right. Tears welled up in her eyes, she was so exhausted. It had been a long and emotionally draining day, running back and forth across town. She sadly walked back to her apartment, clutching the paper with Jeanine's details tightly in her hand. With a heavy heart, she threw herself across her bed and cried herself to sleep.

The following days, Rachel waited in front of the building, desperately hoping to catch Jeanine. She wandered through the parking lot, scanning cars, in search of a familiar one. She approached her neighbors, asking if they had seen Jeanine or knew of her whereabouts. No one seemed to recall the name or face she described. Days turned into a week, and still, no Jeanine.

~ 9 ~

REUNITED

Just as she was about to give up, she recalled her mother saying something about a back entrance Jeanine used to take. Determined to exhaust all possibilities, Rachel searched around the building. Eventually, she stumbled upon a hidden backdoor, marked with a sign, 'Employees Only'.

"I never knew this was back here!!!" Rachel exclaimed.

As she sat near the back entrance, Rachel reflected on the time she and Jeanine shared during their childhood. She reminisced about their adventures and laughter-filled playdates. Emotions stirred within her as she wondered what Jeanine's life was like now. She wondered about the challenges and triumphs she faced over the years and if it was a coincidence that they both ended up at Dream Studios. Rachel sighed as she watched the employees coming and going. She exchanged smiles and brief conversations with some of the residents passing by, hoping they might have some additional information about Jeanine's whereabouts.

Time seemed to stretch and Rachel grew restless. Grabbing a pen from her bag, she decided to fill the hours by jotting down some thoughts and memories in her journal. And then, finally, a familiar car approached. Rachel's heart raced as she watched Jeanine exit her car and grab some bags from her trunk. Overwhelmed by emotion, Rachel could not contain herself, she ran and hugged Jeanine tightly from behind, almost knocking her over.

"What is happening???" Jeanine froze, dropping her bags.

She pried the person's arms from around her and spun around. Her eyes widened as Rachel removed her hood, revealing her face, her face was red and her eyes were filled with tears.

"Rach??? What is going on? Is everything okay???"

"I am so sorry Jeanie! I was so mean to you! My mom told me everything! I am so, so, so, sorry! I misjudged you! Can you please forgive me!!!"

Rachel sobbed uncontrollably as she poured out her heartfelt apology. Jeanine's shock quickly melted into a warm smile, she could see the genuine remorse in her eyes. She wrapped her arms around her long-lost friend and held her tightly.

"Of course, I forgive you, Rach," Jeanine said, her voice filled with love and compassion.

"I appreciate you having the courage to acknowledge your mistake. Do you have time to talk now? We can go up to my place..."

"Yes!" Rachel said excitedly, hugging Jeanine even tighter.

"I have time!"

Rachel helped Jeanine with her bags as they walked up to Jeanine's apartment on the third floor. It was apartment number 3, not 8. Walking inside, Rachel felt a sense of familiarity and comfort, she explained to Jeanine how she had traveled across town the previous day and gotten her information from her mother. Jeanine laughed at Rachel's interaction with her mother, as she put her groceries away.

Settling down into the living room, Rachel and Jeanine exchanged stories, laughs, and tears. They opened up about their experiences over the years. Their highs and lows, their dreams, and the disappointments that shaped their lives. Jeanine opened up about the tragic car accident that took the lives of her husband and children. She shared the determination to rebuild her life after several failed attempts to commit suicide. In turn, Rachel shared her struggles and insecurities, admitting the misjudgments she had harbored. She confessed to the envy and bitterness she had felt, realizing the unfairness of her assumptions. Their friendship instantly rekindled as they sat and talked for hours, tissues covering their laps. Hearing how much Rachel missed her mother's cooking, Jeanine graciously shared some of her mother's soul food with her. Before they knew it, it was dark outside.

"Girl, I have to go to bed. I have class in the morning. Let's talk more tomorrow." Jeanine yawned.

"Awww, ok..." Rachel leaned over and hugged her.

"I still can't believe your mom came to the door with a bat, asking if there was a fire!!!" They fell out in laughter.